## About the Book

In 1614, the Dutch fur trader, Adriaen Block, sailed up the Connecticut River. Friendly Indians greeted him and showed him their beautiful furs. Block named the area New Netherlands and rushed back to Holland with news of his discovery. The same year the Englishman Captain John Smith explored the coastal areas around Cape Cod. *He* named the area New England.

The settlement of the Connecticut River Valley was soon underway, surviving an extended period of Indian wars. Even more valuable than furs to the settlers was the Connecticut's tremendous waterpower, which was later harnessed to make paper and a wide variety of industrial goods.

Elizabeth Gemming highlights the history of the area, which includes Massachusetts, Connecticut, New Hampshire, and Vermont, from the earliest days to the present. She shows how each advance for the area's industrial economy had a harmful effect on the region's abundant wildlife and discusses present attempts to clean up the river with lively anecdotes based on her extensive research. Attractive drawings by Heidi Palmer compliment this informative, highly readable text.

## About the Author

ELIZABETH GEMMING, although not a native New Englander, is a descendant of the *Mayflower* Pilgrims and has lived in the New England area most of her life. She spent many summers at her grandfather's home in New Hampshire, attended Wellesley College in Massachusetts, and currently resides in New Haven, Connecticut.

Elizabeth Gemming is the author of several books for young people, including *Getting to Know New England*. Her husband, Klaus, is a book designer. They have two children, Marianne and Christina.

*About the Artist*

After graduating from Pratt Institute, HEIDI PALMER became a free-lance illustrator. She likes to travel in Europe and the United States and also enjoys farming.

Heidi Palmer lives in Montreal, Canada.

*About the* Getting to Know *Books*

The *Getting to Know* books offer a wide range of exciting and valuable information about countries throughout the world, including the efforts of worldwide organizations. These round-the-world books are designed to give an up-to-date portrait of a land and its people. Concentrating on the everyday life and customs of a region, they incorporate its geography and history, as well as highlight *what's new today*. To keep pace with the fast-changing times, each book is revised periodically.

In addition to this group of international titles, the *Getting to Know* books now include a number of detailed accounts of states and regions within our own country. Everyday life is viewed with a keen historical eye, aimed to give the reader a clear picture of the role each area has played in the development of the nation as a whole. Each book devotes particular attention to the study of historical landmarks which can still be seen today.

Coward, McCann & Geoghegan, Inc.
New York

# Getting to know the
# Connecticut River

## by ELIZABETH GEMMING

### ILLUSTRATED BY HEIDI PALMER

*377114*
*8474*

*J917.4*

# CONTENTS

# 1. THE CONNECTICUT RIVER AND
# THE INDIANS OF THE VALLEY

Among the rivers of America the Connecticut, 410 miles long, is not one of the biggest, but it is surely one of the most scenic. It was born thousands of years ago as a tiny brook that flowed out of a chill pond in what is now northernmost New Hampshire. From this boggy mountain pond the little brook trickled down, down, tumbling over waterfalls, racing along and welcoming tributary streams even wilder than itself.

On its way south the river slowed down and flowed lazily through broad meadows dotted with sugar maples and elms. Each spring the clean sweet waters overflowed their banks to enrich the land. The summer grass grew thick and lush, where someday dairy cows would graze in some of the world's greenest pastures.

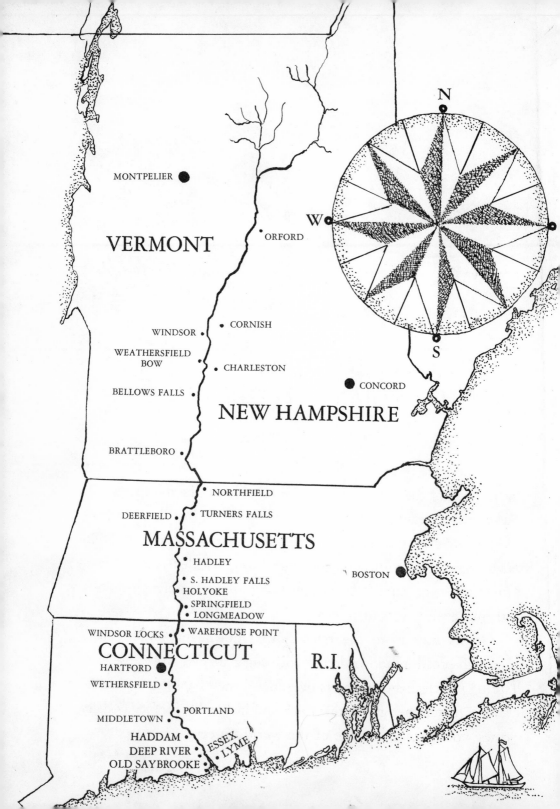

At the place now known as Bellows Falls, the gentle river turned into a torrent as it squeezed through a narrow gorge and plunged over a 50-foot rock ledge. Then, as it entered the region we call the Pioneer Valley of Massachusetts, it grew gentle once more and meandered through a plain where the brown-black soil would one day be planted with vegetables and tobacco. Amid these fields, too, English settlers would build lonely outposts such as Deerfield, doomed to be wiped out twice in Indian raids.

Soon the river broke through a crosswise mountain range of red sandstone where, during the Age of Dinosaurs, 180,000,000 years ago, hundreds of fossil footprints had been laid down in the mud —tracks of little birds, salamanders, giant frogs. and a bird four times the size of the ostrich.

The river glided on and on past groves of trees and open fields that would, in our time, be replaced by brick and granite buildings and the concrete highways and overpasses of metropolitan areas such as Springfield and Hartford. At the place called Longmeadow it reached its widest point—2,100 feet—only to rush again over more rapids below. The river began to move its bed of clay and sand and often changed its course, one year making a bend toward the west, another year curving back toward the east.

Once past a bank of high cliffs, the river rolled toward the sea, emptying into the ocean over a treacherous shifting sandbar just below the surface of the water. Because of this submerged bar, the Connecticut remains to this day the only important American river without a large city or port at its mouth. Now, as in times gone by, waving gray-green salt grasses bow in the breeze beside

11

the river mouth shallows, and even now, only the twin villages of Saybrook and Lyme face each other across the broad estuary.

Without this rather small, very pretty river, half of New England would be parched and stony. But rivers bring life to the dry earth and make it a pleasant home for mankind. Long ago Indians lived on the banks of the lower Connecticut River, which they called *Quinnitukq-ut* or *Quonah-ta-cut*, "the long tidal river." The river was full of fish, and clams and mussels were plentiful near

the mouth. Indian women planted corn, beans, and pumpkins on the natural meadows they called *pocconocks*, and the men planted the sacred tobacco.

The river Indians did not build their wigwams too close to the river, for they knew that each spring, without fail, it would flood the *pocconocks* and renew the fertility of the soil. They had no need to cut down the forests, because the *pocconocks* were farmland enough.

In winter, many Indians journeyed up the river to the far north, to Coös, "the place of the crooked river," which they loved. In Coös (now northern New Hampshire) they hunted deer, moose, squirrels and other small mammals for food and trapped the beaver, otter, wolf, and fox for their fur. In spring, they floated home on the flood current of melting snow, their canoes loaded to the brim with pelts.

Not a soul lived year-round in the evergreen forests of Coös, where the river they called "the Smile of God" was born. But for uncounted generations the lower-river tribes summered in Coös as well, to plant the upland meadows and follow the wild geese south again in the fall. On the way, they assembled at the gorge of the Great Falls, where their sacred carvings covered the face of the rocks. Then, where the river made a great bend by another water-fall, they passed Peskeompskut, their special fishing place, a deep pool that was filled each spring with plump salmon.

After paddling for many miles, they passed the hill that sometimes rumbled from the stirrings of the god Machemoodus. On that hill the river tribes held powwows to pray for victory over their enemy, the dread Pequot tribe that had invaded their beloved country.

As they felt the ocean tide heave under their canoes, the Indians blessed the majestic river that gave them corn, the pelt of the beaver, the salmon and the shad. Silent as always, the "Smile of God" disappeared into the sea.

# 2. WHITE MEN COME TO THE RIVER

One day white men came to the river. They brought tools and trinkets and horses, which the river Indians had never seen. Soon they would build houses foolishly close to the river, whose ways they did not understand. They would move into the Indians' ancient hunting grounds, cut down tall trees for their houses and ships, and drive the abundant wildlife of the valley deeper into the forests. They would dam up the streams to power their sawmills and gristmills and keep the fish from migrating up the river to spawn.

JOHN SMITH

ADRIAEN BLOCK

The first white man to sail up the Connecticut did not stay. He was a Dutch fur trader, Adriaen Block, who discovered it in 1614. In his sloop *Onrust* (*Restless*) he crossed the great sandbar in the spring high water. As the tide weakened and the water seemed less salty, Block realized he was not in a bay but in a river, which he named *De Versche Riviere*, "Freshwater River." After 60 miles, rapids forced him to turn back, but not before friendly Indians had shown him lustrous furs that they had brought down from the north.

Block hurried home to Holland with news of his discovery. A group of merchants in Amsterdam claimed, for Holland, the North American coast from English Virginia to French Acadia (now Maine and Nova Scotia) and called it New Netherlands. That same year, oddly enough, an Englishman, Captain John Smith, had also been exploring the coast, north of Cape Cod. *He* called the land along the coast New England—and neither Block nor Smith knew anything about the other!

Dutchmen from Manhattan Island opened up Freshwater River to trade, and for ten years only Dutch and Indians sailed the Connecticut. Once the Pilgrims had settled in at Plymouth, the Dutch invited them to share in the fur trade, but for some years the Pilgrims were too busy to accept the offer.

Meanwhile, the river Indians were constantly bothered by the Pequots, who had come from the Hudson River country to the west. In 1631 a chief named Wahginnacut thought that since the English newcomers had guns, they might help the river Indians drive out the invaders. He went to see the Pilgrims, who had come to Plymouth on the *Mayflower* eleven years before, and also the Puritans, who had recently arrived from England to found the Massachusetts Bay Colony, a sternly religious settlement around the present city of Boston. He praised his fields of corn, the wild ducks and turkeys of the woodlands and marshes, the fat shad and salmon of the river. He offered them seeds to plant, and eighty beaver pelts a year, if they would only come into the valley.

The Puritans made no promises, but the Pilgrims did decide to look at the river. Pilgrim Edward Winslow became the first Englishman to sail up the Connecticut. The English eventually did side with the river Indians and so won their lasting gratitude and friendship.

SITE OF THE HOUSE OF HOPE

After a band of Dutchmen bought a point of land about 60 miles above the river mouth and opened a trading post they called the House of Hope, a group of Pilgrims promptly set out to build a trading post of their own, upriver from the Dutch. They meant to head off the fur trade before it reached the House of Hope. As the Pilgrim captain sailed by, the Dutch hailed him and asked where he was going.

"Up the river to trade!" he shouted defiantly.

The angry Dutch fired a cannonball across the bow of his ship, but he sailed right on. On the meadow that Winslow had already selected, he quickly put up the ready-made walls and roof of a small house he had brought with him. This post became Windsor, the first permanent English settlement on the Connecticut River.

Before long, people from the Boston area came to the valley, to the old Indian "dancing place" that was to become Wethersfield and also to Windsor. The year 1635 was an exciting one on the Connecticut, for in August a severe hurricane, flood, and tidal wave struck the new settlements. All the corn for their first winter was lost. The Pilgrims at the trading post generously offered the newcomers food and shelter, and in return, the new people simply took

20

over much of the Pilgrims' land. Because the Pilgrims refused to resort to violence to defend their rights, their dream of a New Plymouth on the banks of the Connecticut was abruptly ended.

Also in 1635, an English settlement was founded at the mouth of the river, at Saybrook Point, to await a group of 300 "Lords and Gentlemen" direct from England in the spring of 1636. More and more Massachusetts folk poured into the valley. The first settlement on the east bank of the river, Springfield, was founded. The Reverend Thomas Hooker, from New Towne (now Cambridge), Massachusetts, led his congregation to a spot on the west bank near the Dutch House of Hope. They settled down to raise cattle there, and their cabins were the beginnings of the city of Hartford.

Soon Windsor, Wethersfield, and Hartford decided to break their ties with Massachusetts. They thought the Puritan government in Boston gave too much power to the clergy and not enough to ordinary people. As the Connecticut Colony, these three courageous towns were about to form the first real democracy in America. But first, they had to raise an army, for the Pequots were on the move against them.

Pequot warriors, well-armed and cruel, had began to terrorize the white settlers, ambushing them and burning their houses and barns. The English could not farm, hunt, fish, or even walk to church without risking their lives. In 1637 the Connecticut Colony declared war on the Pequots and, after a bitter struggle, wiped them out. The crushing of the dread Pequots by a few hundred determined Englishmen so impressed the river Indians that there was no open warfare in the valley for the next forty years.

On January 14, 1639, a convention met in Hartford to set up a republic, with governor and lawmakers elected by the people. The vote was granted to all freemen. Their constitution, the Fundamental Orders of Connecticut, was the first written constitution in the world to provide for democratic self-government.

The proud colony grew very fast. In 1640 the Mohegan Indian chief Uncas granted it most of his land. Because of civil war in England, the "Lords and Gentlemen" had never come to Saybrook, so in 1644 the colony took that land over, too. As the population began to increase, the colonists cut down the forests to clear new farmland, and the deer, the beaver, the wild turkey retreated still farther away from the river.

The Dutch were still at the House of Hope, but the English pestered them until they abandoned it. The English took over all Dutch rights in 1654.

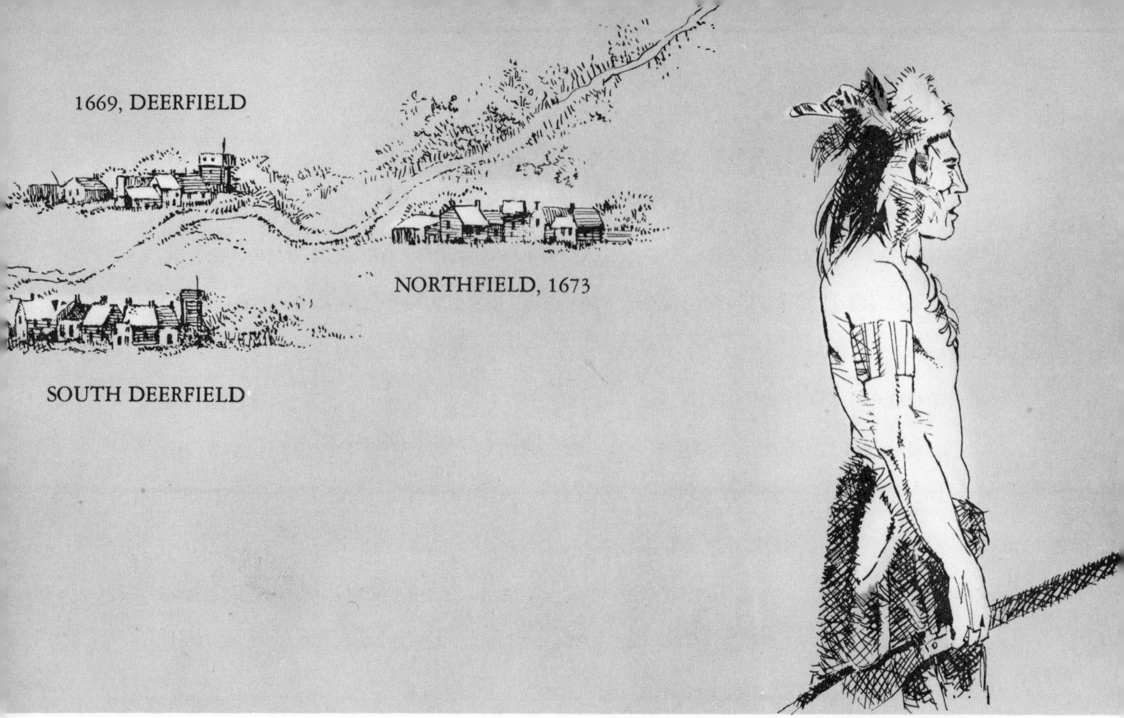

1669, DEERFIELD

NORTHFIELD, 1673

SOUTH DEERFIELD

# 3. INDIAN WARS

After 1660 new settlements were founded in what is now Massachusetts, including Deerfield in 1669 and Northfield in 1673. Beyond, there was nothing but wilderness. Unlike the Indians of the lower river, the Indians of the middle valley had no reason to welcome the white man to their lands.

Trouble began in the summer of 1675 in what is now Rhode Island, when Chief Metacomet, known as King Philip, led an uprising. Though his father, King Massasoit, had welcomed the Pilgrims to Plymouth, he feared for the survival of the Indian way of life and lashed out at the white invaders. Many other tribes were soon drawn into the rebellion.

Philip's braves had long observed the Englishmen's ways, and when they swept out of the forests to attack frontier outposts, the English were no match for their stealthy tactics. At Northfield, which was then nothing but a few log huts and a stockade, the white inhabitants saw eight farmers murdered in the fields and watched helplessly as the Indians killed their cattle, burned their homes, and scattered their grain on the ground. Northfield was hastily abandoned, to become a meeting place for King Philip's river allies.

Hadley, a peaceful farm village, was transformed into military headquarters. Crowded with English and Mohegan soldiers and refugees, it soon ran short of food. One September day a wagon train with a soldier escort was sent north to Deerfield for corn.

Indian scouts in the hills watched the farmers load their carts at Deerfield and turn back. By a swamp along the trail south of town the soldiers put down their guns to snack on wild grapes, not suspecting that in that swamp, their war paint camouflaged by the red and gold autumn foliage, hundreds of Indians lay flat on their stomachs—ambush!

In minutes, sixty-four Englishmen lay dead. The Indians hung the bloodstained clothes of their victims from the trees as a warning and vanished. The people of Deerfield, their nerves shattered, fled south. The muddy stream that trickled through the swamp was given the name it bears to this day: Bloody Brook.

Springfield, a town of forty-five thatch-roofed houses and a brick-and-timber fort, was next. It was attacked and burned, but survived. Little by little the English were learning never to go out after the Indians but to sit tight within their forts and defend them. When hundreds of Indians tried to take Hadley and met unexpected resistance, they slipped into the forest and disappeared for the winter.

27

In March, 1676, large numbers of Indians, near starvation, turned up near Northfield, determined to clear the valley of the white men forever. When the ice melted and the salmon came back to the great fishing place, they rejoiced and prepared to fight. King Philip boldly defied all English offers of peace. The Indians attacked Hadley one more time, only to fall back in defeat before 1,000 soldiers, scouts, and farmers.

By August, 1676, King Philip knew his cause was lost. His wife and only son had been sold as slaves, and he was overcome with grief at the fate of his family and his people. "My heart breaks," he cried out, "now I am ready to die!" He was executed, and his head was carried to Plymouth to be displayed on a day of public thanksgiving.

King Philip's War, in which both sides suffered terrible losses, was over. The English settlers of the Connecticut Valley began to rebuild. But peace did not last. Deerfield, resettled in 1682, found itself in the path of a new enemy: hostile Indians from French Canada and the French themselves. Winter was especially dangerous, for the frozen Connecticut became a fast highway to the south. On snowshoes, and with dogsleds loaded with food and supplies, the French and Indians were able to reach the frontier villages easily.

On the night of February 29, 1704, Deerfield was quiet. Deep snow lay all around, and under the twinkling stars, one watchman fought to keep his eyes open. His head nodded as he listened to a mother singing to her baby, and soon he too was sound asleep.

Before dawn, 200 French and 140 Indians scaled the snow-drifts and palisades and were into the houses before people awoke. Of the 290 people in Deerfield that night, 49 were murdered in their beds or on their doorsteps as they tried to escape.

About 110 captives, among them the minister, John Williams, and his family, were forced to start the 300-mile march on foot to Canada and slavery. Day after day the slow and the weak were killed and left by the wayside, among them Mrs. Williams and her newborn baby.

When the miserable band reached Canada they were divided up among their captors or sold. After two and a half years Parson

Williams was able to ransom and lead 60 of them home to Deerfield. But one daughter, Eunice, seven, was so adored by her French "owners" that they refused to give her up at any price. She received a good French education and married an Indian chief when she grew up. Many years later she came back to Massachusetts to visit. She arrived in full Indian dress, with her husband and an escort of braves, who refused to sleep indoors and set up wigwams in an orchard instead. (Quite a few captive English youngsters remained with the Indians, at least long enough to learn French and tribal languages and the skills of forest life.)

Old Deerfield today is a rather melancholy village of restored eighteenth-century buildings, their timbers weathered to a deep brown, lining a mile-long main street shaded by huge old elms. Eleven houses are open to visitors, and a colonial museum displays furniture, clothing, household and farm equipment, and Indian relics. There you can see a nail-studded wooden house door with holes that were chopped into it by a tomahawk during the massacre of 1704.

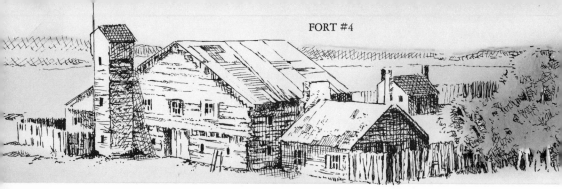

In 1724 Fort Dummer, the pioneer settlement of the upper river, was built (near what is now Brattleboro, Vermont). Forest rangers and trappers began to penetrate the Coös country, and when peace returned to the valley in 1725, eager homesteaders hurried on board canoes and rafts, bound up the river to no-man's-land.

Then, in 1745, Indians killed a farmer out hoeing his corn near Fort Dummer. Once again, a war between England and France back in Europe would bring new terror to the American colonies. Many pioneers abandoned their new homes. A fort at No. 4—new townships were given numbers before names—was quickly garrisoned on the east bank of the river.

(The site of Fort Dummer now lies under water behind a power dam, but a replica of old No. 4—log fort, stockade, great hall, watchtower, and frontier houses—can be visited in summer at Charlestown, New Hampshire.)

During years of peace between 1749 and 1754, the royal governor of New Hampshire, Benning Wentworth, began to grant homesteads west of the river (now the state of Vermont). They were known as the New Hampshire Grants. He wanted to strengthen his claim to the land, and was also in a hurry to get settlers into Coös ahead of the French.

32

But the last French and Indian War broke out in 1754. In October, 1759, Major Robert Rogers and 200 rangers set out for Coös to destroy the village of the St. Francis Indians. After they had done so, they headed back down the Connecticut. By then it was November and cold. Heavy rains had driven game animals from the forests, and supplies sent up from No. 4 never arrived. They survived for a while on nuts, birchbark, lily roots, squirrels, and chipmunks and even gnawed their leather moccasins. Half-dead, Rogers and a few of his men finally got back to the fort to send out rescue canoes with food. For weeks, stragglers came back, but most were never to return at all. Rogers's Rangers made New England safe from the Indians, but at a tremendous price in human lives.

The English conquered Canada in 1760 and the French gave up all their claims in northern America in 1763. Northern New England was no longer in danger of French invasion, so the upper valley was open for English settlement. Governor Wentworth got busy again, and designated 138 townships in just two years! But New York also wanted the land west of the river, and in 1764 King George III of England decided in New York's favor by fixing the boundary between the two provinces at "the western banks of the River Connecticut." The governor of New York pronounced all the New Hampshire Grants illegal and began to regrant the land whether or not it was already occupied. Most homesteaders in the grants refused to get off their land. They did not like to be told what to do by *either* New York or New Hampshire. Maybe this was because many of them had come north from Connecticut, with its heritage of independent self-government. In 1770, a stubborn young Connecticut-born patriot named Ethan Allen organized the Green Mountain Boys in protest, and pioneer farmers, armed with clubs from their woodpiles, went out to battle "Yorker" sheriffs.

On July 4, 1776, all the American colonies, already at war with the British, formally declared independence. On January 15, 1777, in the Westminster courthouse, spirited villagers from the former New Hampshire Grants went a step further and proclaimed themselves entirely "separate, free, and independent" of anyone. At first they called their republic New Connecticut but soon changed its name to Vermont. Then they went off to fight the British with the rest of the Americans.

On July 8 at Windsor, a convention adopted a Vermont constitution which was the first in our nation to abolish slavery and give the vote to all men. Vermont remained free and independent until March 4, 1791, when it joined the Union as the fourteenth state.

A far stranger republic was born in 1796 near the source of the Connecticut River, when three men quietly moved into lands they had bought from the last St. Francis Indian chief. In 1824 the government of New Hampshire was amazed to discover a tucked-away wilderness settlement of nearly 300 people, a hideaway for outlaws without any real government at all. The people called themselves the United Inhabitants of the Indian Stream Territory. The settlement eventually fell apart and was taken over by New Hampshire and renamed Pittsburg—a logging township of 360 square miles that did not join the United States officially until 1842.

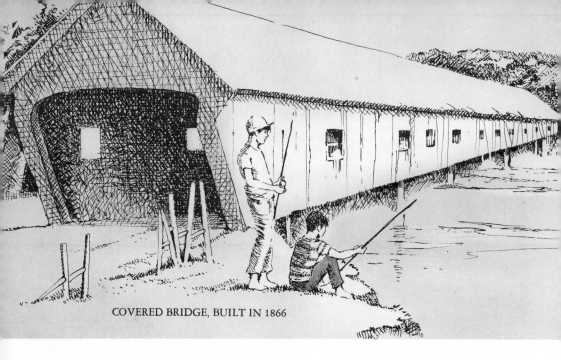

COVERED BRIDGE, BUILT IN 1866

# 4. WAYS TO TRAVEL

Very early, ferries were established on the Connecticut River. The first crossed at Windsor, Connecticut, in 1641. The earliest ferryboats were dugout canoes that also made short trips up and down the river between settlements. (Today two little ferries still serve the river, at Rocky Hill and at Hadlyme, Connecticut.)

Not a single bridge crossed the river until after the Revolutionary War. The first, a toll bridge, was built in 1785 over the gorge at Bellows Falls. A bridge has connected Windsor, Vermont, and Cornish, New Hampshire, since 1796. The first one was lost in a flood, as were two later bridges. The present one, built in 1866, is a covered bridge that is the longest bridge in both states, 460 feet.

A lottery, the usual way to raise money in those days, paid for a bridge at Springfield in 1796. The river was so wide that many people thought they might as well try to span the Atlantic Ocean. The bridge collapsed after nine years and was replaced by a stronger one, 1,230 feet long.

North of the Massachusetts line, New Hampshire owns the Connecticut River, because the legal boundary between New Hampshire and Vermont is the low-water mark on the west bank. The state of New Hampshire must keep all bridges in good repair.

South of Hartford, the river overflowed its banks so often that ferries remained the only way to cross for many years. Not until 1911 did a bridge arch above the mouth of the river between the towns of Saybrook and Lyme—it was the first new link between them since the ferry in 1719!

The first shipping tycoon of the Connecticut River Valley was William Pynchon of Springfield, who arrived in 1635 to trade in furs with the Indians. He built a storage barn below Swift Water (now Warehouse Point, Connecticut), which was for many years the main exchange for cargoes from lower-river sloops to upper-river rafts, canoes, and flatboats.

By the mid-1600's Hartford and other major river towns sent sloops to trade with the West Indies in sugar, rum, and molasses. Middletown became a center for the slave trade—according to the custom of the 1700's no well-to-do New England household was without at least one or two house slaves. By the second half of the eighteenth century Middletown was the river's most important seaport. Large quantities of salted and barreled shad from the river were carried by ship from ports such as Essex to Europe.

Shipbuilding had begun on the river almost as soon as the first settlers arrived. The harbor of Essex, in particular, was always jammed with ships. An Essex shipyard launched the first warship of the U.S. Navy, the *Oliver Cromwell*, just twenty-one days before the Declaration of Independence. The Essex waterfront was raided by the British during the War of 1812, on the night of April 8, 1814. Twenty-eight ships were burned.

The flatboat was the river's most distinctive vessel. It was a long scow with square sails set on a mast around which cargo was stacked up. Brawny boatmen poled the flatboats upstream by means of "the white ash breeze"—not a wind at all, but long white-ash wooden poles they used to shove the boats along!

In the upper-river towns, boisterous, hard-drinking boat crews, known as river gods, sprawled before the fireplaces of local taverns, swapping tales of river heroes, clinking their grog mugs together, and singing loudly into the night. The farther north, the livelier the river landings were, for up north the river was the one route to "everywhere."

Flatboats delivered plows and hoes, grindstones, iron wheel rims, chairs, looms, spinning wheels, salt, sugar, molasses, and rum to the settlers in New Hampshire and Vermont. The boats returned with hides, potash, lumber, and wooden kegs, bowls, tool handles, spools, and shingles made in the little sawmill-workshops that nestled beside the rushing brooks of the upper valley.

As river navigation prospered, it became a nuisance to unload northbound freight at the foot of every waterfall and cart it around on land, only to reload above the rapids. Was there an easier way to get around the falls and rapids?

Yes, there was, and in 1792, on the Connecticut River, the first canals in the Western world were begun. The first to open, at South Hadley Falls in Massachusetts, was cut through solid rock. The water level was raised or lowered by two big water wheels on either side of an elevator contraption that took on boats or rafts one at a time. A second canal opened at Turners Falls in 1800. This canal destroyed the Indians' salmon pool of Peskeompskut, for it prevented the fish from leaping the falls to spawn. (Mill dams and canals blocked the spring migration during which salmon and shad, through some mysterious homing instinct, leave the ocean and fight their way upstream to lay their eggs in the cold fresh-water pools where they were born.)

A short canal with nine locks and a dam was finished at Bellows Falls in 1802. By 1810 three canals in Vermont permitted boats to reach Fifteen Mile Falls, 220 miles north of Hartford. Yet not until 1829 did a navigation canal bypass the troublesome Enfield Rapids, the Indians' "Swift Water." (The canal was built too late to be profitable, for the efficient railroad was about to come to the valley.)

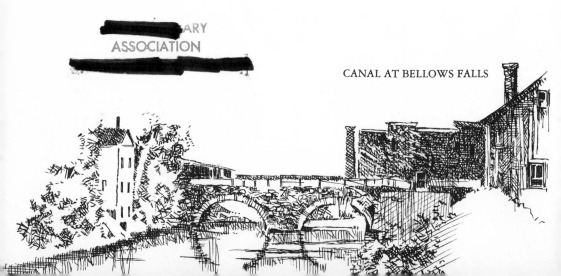

CANAL AT BELLOWS FALLS

FULTON'S *CLERMONT*

SAMUEL MOREY

The steamboat was invented in the Connecticut River Valley. Most people think that Robert Fulton invented the steamboat, but the real "father of steamboat navigation in America" was Captain Samuel Morey of Orford, New Hampshire. In 1790 he tried out a small paddle-wheeler on the river. In 1793 his steamboat *Aunt Sally* made such a good run that he hurried to New York to look for people who might invest money in his invention. While there, he met Fulton, who looked at his plans and did not seem particularly impressed with them.

On his way home Morey made America's first long-distance steamboat trip, 160 miles through Long Island Sound and up the Connecticut to Hartford. He took out patents and planned to build boats on a grand scale, but his backers never gave him any of the money they had promised. By 1807, when Fulton's famous *Clermont* steamed up the Hudson River, people had forgotten all about Samuel Morey. He always suspected that Fulton had stolen his invention while pretending to criticize it.

In 1824 steamboats went into service between Hartford and New York. The handsome paddle-wheeler *Oliver Ellsworth* was a typical boat—127 feet long, with ugly smoke belching from its stacks, but very elegant all the same. It had cabins for sixty, a gentlemen's bar in the bow, and a covered promenade for ladies in the stern.

Because of the narrow locks and canals, it was never profitable to run steamboats north of South Hadley Falls, but popular steamboats flourished between Springfield and Hartford until the railroad linked the two cities in 1844. Fashionable New Yorkers came to Connecticut for their summer vacations by steamboat, and the same boats carried tons of "brownstone" back down the river from the quarries at Portland, Connecticut, to build New York town houses. In the late 1800's rambling hotels with broad verandas and carved "gingerbread" trim overlooked the river and the Sound.

(The Goodspeed Opera House, built in 1877, still perches on the riverbank at East Haddam. It looks very much like the old-time hotels, and in summer it stages old-fashioned musical comedies.)

At Nook Farm in Hartford, where he lived for twenty years, Mark Twain recalled the Mississippi River steamboat days of his childhood as he wrote *Tom Sawyer* and *Huckleberry Finn.* The house, a big red-brick Victorian home that even looks a little like a riverboat, with turrets and decklike porches, is open to visitors. (If you would like to take a summertime boat trip on the river, you can take the modern excursion boat *Yankee Clipper* or the paddle-wheeler *River Queen* from East Haddam or Saybrook Point.

For many years, working steamboats have been gone from the river, but commercial shipping between Hartford and Long Island Sound is busier than ever. Diesel ships and tankers now carry more than 3,000,000 tons of cargo each year, about half of which is fuel oil bound for the Hartford area.

The main reason why steamboating declined was the coming of the railroad. About 1829, people first thought seriously of laying iron rails for "steam-propelled stagecoaches." Some people believed that God had never meant human beings to travel at the

dreadful speed of 15 miles per hour. Farmers worried that their cows would be scared by the noise of the trains and would stop giving milk. Steamboat companies fought the competition. Toll-road builders argued that gentlemen ought to travel in style in their own coaches, not in sooty steam trains where they might be herded in with common ruffians!

But nothing could stop the railroad. The first train came to Springfield in 1838. The first tracks along the river were laid from Springfield to Hartford in 1844. Springfield, at the crossroads of the east-west rail line between Boston and Albany and the north-south river traffic, quickly grew into a great railroad center. In 1853 a locomotive first tooted into the Coös country, and in 1887, a train rolled nearly to the Canadian border at Colebrook, New Hampshire.

Wherever the iron horse went, it brought prosperity and jobs, just as the flatboats and steamboats had done before. People were needed at every depot to feed and water the locomotive .The trains gobbled lots of firewood, so more trees were quickly and carelessly cut. Wild animals of the woodlands withdrew deeper and deeper into the dark forests and hardly ever ventured into the noisy new settlements.

Below Hartford, the powerful Connecticut Steam Boat Company managed to block the railroad for years. Finally, in 1868, the Connecticut Valley Railroad laid tracks from Hartford south to connect with the steamers at Saybrook. But the steamboat companies still fought the railroad, and it failed.

(In 1968 a group of railroad lovers repaired four miles of Valley RR tracks between Essex and Deep River and restored an old locomotive and passenger cars for sightseeing trips that connect with the excursion boats at Deep River.)

In recent years American railroads have failed as trucks and airlines have taken over much freight and passenger business. Some areas have suffered greatly over the loss of rail service, for example, northwestern Massachusetts, New Hampshire, and Vermont, which had no passenger trains at all after 1966. Then, on a rainy night in September, 1972, the railroad returned to the upper Connecticut Valley. When the first of the daily sleeper trains between Washington, D.C., and Montreal, Canada, passed through rundown depots sometime between midnight and dawn, red, white, and blue flags were hung out, high school bands played salutes, and valley folk turned out in the darkness to cheer!

# 5. YOUR OLD DAM'S GONE

From earliest days gristmills and sawmills have made use of the natural waterpower of streams. Some mills in New England soon began manufacturing small wooden articles from the lumber they cut. Connecticut Valley people were clever and inventive, and abundant waterpower was there for the taking, so they began building dams and canals to harness the river for larger-scale manufacturing. Perhaps people didn't realize that these dams and canals would block the shad and salmon migrations and drive the fish from the river. Maybe they didn't care that much, and besides, the fish seemed more than plentiful.

49

Industry had its start in the valley shortly before 1830 in what is now Holyoke, Massachusetts. A millowner tried to coax river water into a small canal to turn the 4,000 spindles that processed his cotton. In the 1840's a company built a dam to harness the power behind South Hadley Falls. Finished in 1848, it was to be the greatest man-made source of waterpower in the world. Newspaper dispatches tell the story:

10 A.M. Gates just closed; water filling behind dam.
12 M. Dam leaking badly.
2 P.M. Stones of bulkhead giving way to pressure.
3:20 P.M. Your old dam's gone.

A new dam, built the following year, fortunately held fast. Today there are seventeen dams on the Connecticut, either linked with electric dynamos for power or serving pulp and paper mills.

In 1853 the first of Holyoke's famous paper mills were opened. Papermaking requires two things: soft water and wood pulp. Each spring the upper river was black with logs cut during the winter and hauled to the banks of frozen streams to wait for "ice-out." When the snow in the uplands melted and the Connecticut held 150 times its normal amount of water, loggers formed "boxes" by fastening 60-foot tree trunks together with planks and wooden pins. Eighteen boxes made a "raft," to be oared or poled down river. Logging was extremely dangerous work, and many loggers were killed. For years, until blocked by modern dams, the Connecticut River log drives were the world's longest, and millions of logs were floated down to the mills.

In Holyoke a three-canal system was built to link up with the South Hadley Falls dam and recycle river water three times over. These canals conveniently brought clean water to the doorsteps of the paper mills, but they also made it easy for the mills to dump chemical wastes right back into the river. Of the 3,700 industrial plants on the river basin in 1972, only 20 were paper mills. And yet they are the prime contributors to the pollution of the Connecticut River, according to a recent study. The study shows that all of the industries would have to spend a total of 648 million dollars to bring the river up to the Federal pollution control standards—if they began acting immediately. Of this 170 million dollars, almost one-fourth of the total would have to be spent by the paper industry.

Besides supplying the paper industry, lumber from the northern forests now supplies several furniture factories in the valley. The valley's most famous "product" is probably insurance policies, for Hartford, home of some thirty-five firms, is America's "insurance city." Most of the world's jet aircraft engines are made in East Hartford.

Since colonial times the valley has manufactured a wide variety of notions, hardware, and tools. Foremost among these are firearms for sport and war. Modern assembly-line methods originated early in the nineteenth century in Hartford's gun factories, where interchangeable precision gun parts were made that make repairs easy. Samuel Colt patented the first pistol in 1835, and Colt's Hartford factory was mass-producing guns by 1848. The world's first revolver, the Colt .45, was also made there. The Colt factory still makes six-shooters and made the M-16 rifles used in Vietnam.

The Springfield Armory, oldest in the nation, began making muskets in 1795. There Canadian-born John C. Garand invented the M-1 rifle used in the Second World War and Korean War. The armory was shut down in 1968, and today it houses a gun museum containing 10,000 firearms.

SPRINGFIELD ARMORY

SAMUEL COLT

The Connecticut Valley is by no means all industrial, though. It is one of our most fertile farming regions. The rich loamy soil of the floodplain, the river's gift, is the secret of its fertility. Good soil is one of our earth's most valuable resources. Yet as early as 1810, in Coös, the rich topsoil laid down over centuries began to wash away after people cut the forests carelessly and hastily. They did not realize that tree roots anchor soil and hold in precious moisture while at the same time soaking up excess water from the ground. The Connecticut and its wild tributaries soon took revenge in sudden washouts and frequent floods.

The hurricanes of 1635, 1815, and 1938 caused disastrous flooding. The worst flood of modern times struck the valley in March, 1936, when four feet of snow in the mountains melted in just four warm rainy days. Today flood-control dams help protect the valley from such disasters, and sensible forest management is important, too. (Some scientists, on the other hand, do not think that floods are necessarily bad, since they renew the natural richness of the land. The trouble is only that people insist on building too *close* to the river.)

At any rate, thanks to the great river, the valley produces 200,000,000 pounds of potatoes each year, as well as other vegetables such as corn, tomatoes, lettuce, asparagus, and, most of all, onions.

Dairying is a leading agricultural occupation all up and down the valley. The sweet meadows of the upper valley, in Vermont especially, are famous for fresh milk and fine cheese. You'll often hear that Vermont has (or once had) more cows than people!

About 1840 Vermont also had more than five sheep for every human being, at a time when New England flocks numbered more than a million animals. Hardly anyone in the valley raises sheep

today, but at one time it was one of New England's major occupations. It all began when an American diplomat named William Jarvis retired from Portugal to Weathersfield Bow, Vermont, bringing with him a flock of fine Spanish Merino sheep. Before long, all the folk in the tiny "bow" village in a bend of the Connecticut River were raising sheep, and sheep raising for wool quickly spread throughout New England.

The most famous and unusual of all valley crops is shade-grown
tobacco, for cigar wrappers. (The first cigars ever made in the
United States were rolled at South Windsor, Connecticut, in 1801
by a farmer's wife named Mrs. Prout, who peddled them from a
wagon.) This delicate tobacco is very expensive to grow because it
must be tended every step of the way by hand. It does bring the
highest cash return per acre of any farm crop in the nation—in a
recent year $24,000,000.

The plants are sheltered from damage in summer hailstorms by white gauze canopies that also shield them from burning sunlight and re-create the hot but hazy climate of the tropics. Each ripe leaf is harvested by hand and hung to dry and cure in airy brown barns scattered here and there in the flat fields, in both Connecticut and Massachusetts.

The Indians smoked the leaves of a small-leaved native tobacco plant and also made a drink from it. They taught the first settlers how to grow it, and later the English brought in a broad-leaved variety from Virginia. The Cuban variety grown today was first cultivated under gauze about 1900.

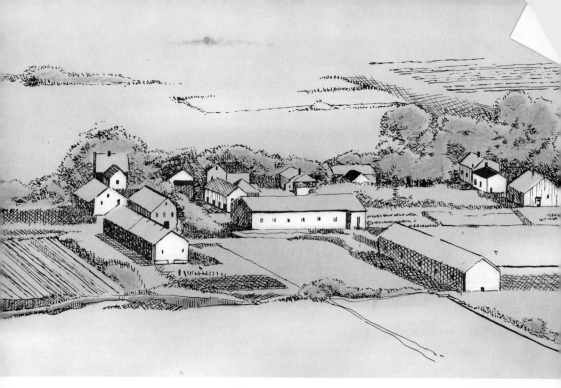

# 6. RIVER RECOVERY

The Connecticut Valley is a beautiful place to visit, and today the best way to come is by car. Highway I-93 speeds you through New Hampshire to the upper valley, and highway I-91 runs up the river from Hartford north—its Vermont stretch is one of our nation's most scenic fast roads. Actually, these superhighways may threaten the peace and natural beauty of the valley as crowds of tourists pour in and need places to eat and sleep, boat, camp, and swim. For the river, once badly polluted, is being cleaned up. It is hoped that the entire river will be clean enough for swimming by 1976.

SENATOR ABRAHAM RIBICOFF

Because of industry, the Connecticut was one of our first polluted rivers—not much of an honor. (Hartford banned the use of river water for drinking nearly 100 years ago.) Five years ago the river smelled so awful from sewage, factory wastes, and garbage that only rats ventured near the banks. Today, the U.S. "Pure Waters" law requires river towns to stop dumping and, in many cases, build special waste-disposal plants. If left to itself, in fact, a strong, life-supporting river such as the Connecticut will eventually clean itself by diluting pollutants and breaking down wastes bacterially. Near the mouth, tides bathe it twice a day.

In 1970 Senator Abraham Ribicoff of Connecticut, who was worried about safeguarding the restored beauty of the valley, asked Congress to establish a system of national parklands along the river: a Gateway Unit from Saybrook to Haddam, a Mount Holyoke unit in Massachusetts, and an 80-mile Scenic River Unit in Coös. Trailer parks, marinas, cheap cottages, drive-ins, and unneeded dams were not to be allowed. The Senate approved the Gateway Unit in 1972, but local citizens, still concerned about public recreation vs. natural preservation, have recently turned it down.

The Connecticut River basin is a land area of about 11,260 square miles, with a population of about 2,000,000. Nine-tenths of these people live between Hartford, Connecticut and Springfield, Massachusetts. Much of the valley is heavily forested today, and one-quarter of it is farmland. There are close to 4,000 factories in the valley, with pulp and paper mills expanding in the north. Because it drops 2,650 feet from its source to the sea, the fast-flowing river is now important mainly as a producer of power. Multimillion-dollar hydroelectric plants can provide plenty of jobs, as well as pay high taxes to communities that need the money.

Unfortunately, such power plants use river water to cool their generators and discharge the heated water back into the river, causing thermal pollution. The river's temperature goes up, and fish, larvae, and snails that live in the river may die. In summer, the river surface may reach 90 degrees or more, and that is too hot for all but tropical fish. Experiments have not yet shown exactly how harmful thermal pollution is, since the river cools

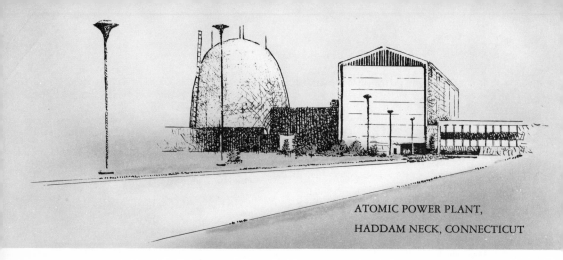

ATOMIC POWER PLANT,
HADDAM NECK, CONNECTICUT

again a few miles past a power plant, but no doubt it is a serious problem.

An atomic power plant at Haddam, Connecticut, releases hot water into the river that probably endangers the lives of young shad returning to the sea in late summer. A spectacular new nuclear power plant at Vernon, Vermont, has been idle as angry citizens try to sue to keep it from opening. Everyone agrees that we must find new sources of power and energy, for coal and oil transportation costs are just too high. Atomic power seems ideal, yet the cost of developing and running atomic power plants that will allow the river to stay healthy will be tremendous. People of the valley must decide whether they are willing to help pay the price of caring for the river that has made the valley the prosperous and lovely place that it is.

Environmental action groups are busy today challenging the licenses of power companies, in order to force them to help restore the Atlantic salmon and the shad to the Connecticut. The first dams and canals, as you know, caused the fish to disappear, and modern dams present hopeless obstacles. Fish ladders—series of pools arranged stepwise—can be constructed to help fish leap over the dams on their way to spawn upstream.

Shad have already returned below Holyoke dam. The power company that owns the dam has operated a fish lift since 1955, a kind of elevator that raises the shad to the top of the dam and dumps them out to swim the 35 miles up to their spawning pools at Turners Falls—the Indians' ancient Peskeompskut!

The Atlantic salmon and the shad are consided delicious treats today, and it is hard to believe that these fish were once so plentiful in Connecticut that an old law forbade people from feeding them to their servants more than three times a week. People used fish to fertilize corn hills, Indian fashion. Shad was scorned as "Connecticut River pork," and people who did eat it dined in secret for fear their neighbors would think they were too poor to afford meat.

Now 1,000,000 baby salmon are stocked in the river yearly, and after three to five years in the salty Atlantic they may return to the freshwater river to spawn. Today's yearly spring shad run at the river mouth averages 1,000,000 and commercial shad fishermen now work in the estuary. Biologists hope the number of

shad can be doubled in the future, for fish is one of the world's most nutritious foods.

For years our land has been soaked with pesticides and pollutants, and creatures of sea, river, earth, and air have been sickened or destroyed. All along the coast, salt marshes are dying. One of our most magnificent birds, the osprey or fish hawk, may die out

from eating fish that have absorbed poisons such as DDT (which has finally been banned, perhaps too late).

One of the world's largest breeding colonies of these handsome, eaglelike, brown-and-white birds used to be at Old Lyme at the mouth of the Connecticut—in the 1950's there were about 150 nests. But in 1971 there were only 3 nests, with just two healthy young ospreys, and 1973 may be the last year that ospreys will ever nest at Old Lyme.

Mother ospreys have been laying eggs containing deformed chicks or eggs with shells so thin that they quickly break. A few years ago a young student from Connecticut tried a daring scheme to save the river osprey colony. He brought healthy eggs and downy chicks up from the Maryland shore and placed them in nests at Old Lyme. The river ospreys, good parents, accepted them and raised the babies as their own. So the osprey may survive—or it may not. The Maryland ospreys, apparently healthy, have recently begun to show signs of sickness. Only time will tell. If you have ever been lucky enough to see an osprey cruise, circle, and drop

suddenly to seize a fish from the water, you will understand how sad it will be if these wonderful birds disappear from the earth.

Several summers ago, a group of grade-school pupils and their teachers from a school in East Haddam, Connecticut, got to know the river very well. They made a 380-mile canoe trip down the Connecticut River as a science project. At first, up north, the river was crystal clear, but before long the children were paddling through scum and raw sewage. Some got sick. They passed garbage dumps, junk-auto graveyards, dead fish, heaps of wood chips, and water dyed purple, copper, and green from factory wastes.

And yet there were some places where the river was edged thickly with bright green trees. Sheltered from the noises of traffic, the young voyagers could hear the songs of birds in a blue sky. They gazed at the sweet meadows, lazy oxbow bends, and majestic cliffs and gasped at the churning rapids. Here and there they

spotted beavers or otters, ducks, perhaps a deer, and they began to fall in love with the river.

They came home determined to help save the Connecticut and sent long reports to lawmakers. They made more trips and got involved in clean-up and research projects. If we all learn to care, and learn what to do to help, the Connecticut River, its wildlife, its historic villages, and its valuable natural resources can be preserved.

What *is* a river? As one boy said when he came back from the canoe trip, "It's life running along!"

# IMPORTANT DATES IN THE CONNECTICUT RIVER'S HISTORY

1614—Adriaen Block, a Dutch fur trader, discovers the river.

About 1621—The Dutch open up the river to trade in furs with the Indians.

About 1633—Edward Winslow, a Plymouth Pilgrim, is the first Englishman to sail up the river.

Spring, 1635—Puritans from Massachusetts found Wethersfield and settle at Windsor (Connecticut), where the Pilgrims already run a trading post.

August, 1635—Windsor is struck by a disastrous hurricane.

May, 1636—Springfield, the first settlement on the east bank of the river, is founded.

June, 1636—The Reverend Thomas Hooker and his congregation arrive on the river and found Hartford.

1639—The three towns' of Windsor, Wethersfield, and Hartford, as the Connecticut Colony, adopt a constitution, the Fundamental Orders of Connecticut.

1641—The river's first ferry is established at Windsor.

1654—The English take over all Dutch claims on the river.

1669—Pioneers found Deerfield (Massachusetts).

1673—Northfield (Massachusetts) is founded on the northern frontier.

1675–76—King Philip's War.

February 29, 1704—The Deerfield massacre.

1724—Fort Dummer, first permanent settlement on the upper river, is founded.

1745—Fort No. 4 on the east bank is garrisoned.

1749—Governor Benning Wentworth of New Hampshire begins granting land to settlers in what is to become Vermont.

1754–63—The last French and Indian War.

1760—The English conquer French Canada.

1763—The French give up all claims in the New World.

1775–81—The War of Independence.

June, 1776—The U.S. Navy's first warship, the *Oliver Cromwell*, is launched at Essex on the Connecticut River.

January 15, 1777—The people of Wentworth's New Hampshire Grants declare themselves a free and independent republic.

1785—The first bridge spans the river, at Bellows Falls.

1792—The first navigation canals and locks in the western world are begun on the Connecticut River.

1793—Samuel Morey tries out his steamboat on the river.

April 8, 1814—British sailors raid Essex and burn twenty-eight ships.

1824—Steamboat service between Hartford and New York begins.

1838—The railroad comes to the river, at Springfield.

1844—Springfield and Hartford are linked by rail.

1848—The huge new dam at South Hadley Falls bursts and is replaced the following year.

1853—Holyoke's first paper mills open.

1868—The Connecticut Valley Railroad wins the right to lay tracks from Hartford to Saybrook.

1911—The first bridge is built across the mouth of the river between Saybrook and Lyme.

March, 1936—The worst flood of modern times strikes the valley.

1966—A major discovery of dinosaur tracks is uncovered at Rocky Hill, Connecticut.

1970—Senator Ribicoff of Connecticut proposes a system of national parklands to safeguard the river valley.

September, 1972—Railroad service is restored to the central and upper valley after an absence of six years.

June, 1973—A survey of the Connecticut River Valley predicts that cleaning up its polluted air and water will cost towns and industries in the four river states more than $1.3 billion by 1980.

Present—As valley residents discover just how seriously the beauty and health of their river have been endangered, they are joining conservation groups, writing to lawmakers, and pitching in to work on local clean-up committees. Though there is still much to be done, these concerned citizens of all ages can be proud of their first efforts, because the Connecticut River is on the way to recovery.

# INDEX